PURPOSE UNSTOPPABLE

Tiffany M. Hill

Atlanta, Georgia

PURPOSE UNSTOPPABLE

ISBN: 978-0-578-53870-9

Printed in the United States of America

Visit the author's social media outlets:

Instagram: @purposeunstoppable

Facebook: @purposeunstoppablepu

Cover image design: Charles Hill

Published by

FHA Books, LLC

@FHABOOKS

DEDICATION

This book is dedicated to the one true and living Almighty God.

Dear Father,

I cannot explain with words how grateful I am to you Lord; you have truly changed my life from your presence and my continued growing in you. There's no way that I can do life or anything without you, you made yourself so very real to me and it means more to me than my words can express. The fact that you cared for me throughout my life, despite the times I overlooked you, you have always been there. I thank you for the many experiences we've shared together and I look forward to many more to come. I thank you for hearing me the many times I would cry out to you, and you would understand when no one else could; and the times I did not have the words to express, you would know and would still provide a response to comfort me every time. Without you giving me this book, encouraging and leading me by your spirit, it wouldn't have been possible. I love you Lord, because you first loved me. I will not turn back. I will continue to serve you all the days of my life and I will share with the whole world who you are and what you have done for me.

Your Daughter,

Tiffany M. Hill

Acknowledgments

I sincerely thank you with love;

To my Husband Charles, thank you for your prayers, continued support and understanding throughout this journey, it has meant so much to me. The many late nights and early mornings you were there to encourage me to keep going and not give up.

To my beautiful daughters, thank you for never giving up on me. You've been patient and supportive and I am blessed that God chose me to mother you.

To my siblings, thank you for your prayers and support. I love you dearly.

To my Parents; Mother- Edward & Venus Winn, Daddy- George & Lisa Feagins Sr., thank you for your prayers, encouragement and support that you've always shown me, you have crossed mountains to support me, I am very grateful and blessed to have you as my parents.

To my *Uncle Pastor Rodney Feagins, Prophet Frederick Spidell, Reverend Gerald F. Jones, Reverend Emma Rolland & Reverend Edna Dillard*, thank you for your prayers and leadership. I also thank you for being a special part of my life encouraging me to continue walking with and following our Lord and Savior Jesus Christ.

To my *Women's Daily Walk Family*, thank you all for your prayers, encouragement and support.

To *Freddie Allen & Kim Wilson*, thank you for your support and encouragement.

To my *Extended Family & Friends*, thank you for your prayers, support and love.

Contents

Introduction

Before God changed and transformed my life, I experienced low self esteem, depression and insecurity. I was ashamed of my past, confused and lost about my direction and purpose in life and frustrated with what the future held for me. I had a desire to know who I really was and what I was supposed to be doing. there was something inside of me telling me that there was something more. I tried finding it by asking people around me, seeking mentors and by obtaining degrees. I can recall driving in my car one day, thinking to myself what was I going to do next with no solid direction about life and I said, "I guess I'll go back to school." I couldn't figure it out. I then began settling in the routine of life and that left me feeling stuck. I would pick up my children from school, I would go home after having a full day at work, while preparing dinner I would converse with my family about their day, my Husband is usually helping with homework and dinner, and after this we're preparing for the next day and back at it again until the weekend. I would pray sparingly or when I needed something, and I would only read the Bible on Sunday's at church, and that wasn't often because my family and I gradually stopped attending church due to my lack of interest. I felt as though something was missing. I can remember after some of the church services that we attended I would ask my Husband to explain the sermon once we made it to the car. I had no desire or interest in attending church; and after speaking with my Husband we decided that we were not going back.

After three years of not attending church, in the third year, 2016, I began to feel an inner pull towards the direction of God. I would often feel as if I had one foot in and one foot out with one foot leaning more towards God than the other. I cannot really explain this pulling feeling I had, but this is the best way that I can describe it. One day, after coming home from work, I began searching YouTube. Once my routine was done for the day and my children were in bed and asleep, I would be up late at night watching videos. As I began searching for videos, I can recall watching a particular video that blew my mind. After this I became very intrigued with what people were sharing on their videos about their dreams and experiences with God. As I continued to watch videos for several weeks, I believe God was speaking directly to me. I would literally be up until 3:00 a.m. and would have to be up for work by 6:30 a.m. I was tired many days, but excited all at the same time to get back home to find another video to hear what God had done in someone else's life.

Then, in the month of December 2016, when everyone was asleep, the Holy Spirit began to draw me to Him; I went to find the quietest place in my home which was my closet. While sitting on the floor, I began to seek God without having any thoughts about how others told me to pray to seek Him. I mean I went for it ya'll! The best way I knew how. I started to have real and true conversations from the depths of my very soul pouring everything out to God. As I began weeping deeply, with tears running profusely down my face, the warmth of Jesus' presence invaded my space. In that very moment, I immediately knew that I couldn't stand in His presence because I was filthy and dirty of the things I had done. It was as if, God was making me remember the things I had done; things I thought I had forgotten about. He lead me to confess my most deepest and secret sins. From the sins I was embarrassed to confess out loud to myself, to the smallest things that meant so much to Him. I immediately asked God to forgive me of my sins and I repented.

Shortly, after this experience, which I refer to as an awakening, I realized I was more aware of God's presence around me. He literally lifted the scales from my very own eyes and I was able to see Him everywhere. I recall walking in the grocery store seeing God in His people; His presence was felt outdoors, around the trees, birds and in the wind. This was amazing! After this, I realized that God is definitely with us at all times.

After experiencing my awakening, I realized that there's something more to the Christian life that I did not have prior to experiencing my awakening. I was initially saved and baptized at the age of thirteen, but this experience was different. I was truly changed and transformed by His presence and from the moment that I was awakened I have continued to remain and have grown in God. He has set me free from the bondage of low self-esteem, depression and insecurity, the shamefulness of my past, my confusion and frustrations. I have stepped out by faith in response to God to fulfill the calling and purpose on my life. I am committed to following Jesus Christ no matter the cost.

As I share my story with you throughout this book, I want you to know that we are not perfect. Romans 3:23 (NIV) states "for all have sinned and fall short of the glory of God." Just as God accepted me as I returned back to Him, He will do the same thing for you. It's never too late to come back to the Lord, no matter how far off track you may think you are. If you're still here living and breathing on earth, then God has His arms wide open and He's waiting right now to welcome you back home. I encourage you to chase after God like never before. Be Purpose Unstoppable for the Kingdom of God, by fulfilling the calling and purpose God has placed upon your life, with boldness only to glorify our Lord and Savior Jesus Christ!

"Time is never wasted, when in the presence of God."

~Tiffany M. Hill

1

Developing a Relationship with God

~ John 15:5 (NIV) ~

"I am the vine; you are the branches. If you remain in me and I in you, you will bear much fruit; apart from me you can do nothing.

After experiencing my awakening, I started developing my personal relationship with God. It was initially something very new for me. I was actually applying effort to the relationship with the power of me making a choice to do so. Before experiencing my awakening, I had never made a conscious effort and I did not quite understand that I could connect with God in the way of a relationship. After my awakening, through the Holy Spirits teaching and leading, I was able to experience developing a relationship with God. And it was exciting! I'll try to explain it. It was as if I had met a guy for the first time; a guy who I really wanted to get to know. The more we were around one another, I wanted to know him more and more. I wanted to spend a lot more time with him. Eventually I fell in love and I told everyone I knew about him. I couldn't stop talking about him. Then he proposed, I become engaged, and then married. Now I can't live without Him. Lol! Praise God!

The basis and the foundation of our Christian life start with a relationship with our Lord and Savior Jesus Christ. It is rooted and wrapped in love. God's love is so great for us that He gave His only son as a sacrifice to die for our sins. It is through Gods love for us that we love Him. When we build a personal relationship with God, we began to experience His love for us. We see ourselves from His lenses as to who we are in Christ, and what He has done for us through His son Jesus.

In developing your relationship with God, it involves communication, association, intimacy and nearness. I believe, in order to have a successful relationship with anyone, such as in a marriage or in a friendship, two of the needed things they must have are communication and an emotional connection. This is how we also are to connect with God. Our emotional connection with God allows us to share our personal thoughts and feelings that no one else could understand if we told them. Our communication is tailored around bonding with God. There's an exchange going on that is nourished in love, continual communication and trust. This is what God wants for us and Him to have together continually. When we do not acknowledge and have a continual relationship with God, it is as if we are living in a home with a person who loves us more than we could ever imagine; a person who provides for us in every area of our lives and is being ignored visibly and verbally.

John 15:5 (NIV) states "I am the vine; you are the branches. If you remain in me and I in you, you will bear much fruit; apart from me you can do nothing." This scripture tells us that our fruit grows only when we are attached and connected to the vine. Fruit cannot grow to become fruit, like a good sweet juicy plum, without being planted and fed from the vine itself. When we are not connected to the vine as the branch our fruit cannot be eaten; it's tossed away and we are saying to God we can do everything without Him. This is not what God wants for us, He wants us to stay and remain in Him and not apart from Him. When we remain in Him, our relationship with God grows and matures, but it is not intended to stay in the same place. For instance, as we grew as children, we began in the infancy stage being held and shortly thereafter we began to crawl, walk and we eventually began to run. This means our growth in God should be moving into a deeper understanding and more trusting relationship that continues to grow stronger and stronger each day.

While on your Christian journey, I encourage you to develop your relationship with God. Determine ways you can seek to grow more in God. Our goal is to become more like Jesus Christ.

Find Time to Spend With God

~ Matthew 6:33 (NIV) ~

But seek first his kingdom and his righteousness, and all these things will be given to you as well.

In order for us to continue developing and strengthening our relationship with God, it is important for us to find the time to spend with Him by scheduling our time, especially if your life is as busy as my life is with having a family. The more time we spend with God through prayer and reading the Bible is when we tap into a higher level of intimacy and closeness that brings about an awareness of His presence in our lives. We learn of Him in different ways as the relationship continues to grow and it allows us to bear fruit that will show up in and through our lives by abiding in Him. Galatians 5:22-23 (NIV) says "But the fruit of the Spirit is love, joy, peace, forbearance, kindness, goodness, faithfulness, gentleness and self-control. Against such things there is no law."

In scheduling time to spend with God daily, we must be intentional. It's just as if you're scheduling time for an important occasion or event in your life that you cannot miss. However, this appointment with God is far more important and on a consistent basis. God wants our best, and He wants us to be in fellowship with Him on a daily basis. This is not just when we need something or when we are having a hard time in life. He wants us to make Him a part of our everyday lives. We do this by including, acknowledging and reverencing God by finding the time in our day to spend with Him.

As I began spending time with God, I was all over the place initially, I would miss reading the Bible in the morning, I would then pray at night. I tried to read the Bible after putting my children to bed and I found myself exhausted and sleepy or vice versa for the next day. This is when I discovered that I needed to get it together and give God my best by finding the time in my schedule for Him. My goal was to have uninterrupted time with the Lord and I wanted to take my relationship with God serious. This meant that I needed to make some changes with managing my time and rearranging my schedule to incorporate some form of consistency for prayer and reading the Bible.

My day included working a fulltime, 40 hour per week, job (working over some days), cooking when I arrived home (most days), completing homework task with my children, preparing my girls for bed and finally spending one on one time with my Husband. As you can see, my day appeared to be full. So I began praying, asking the Lord to help me identify the time to spend with Him, being that most of my day was spent at work. The Lord answered my prayer and led me to take out a blank piece of paper. As I took out a piece of paper, I started to chart the time I woke up in the mornings to the time I went to bed. I tried squeezing time in during my day in between my early mornings and late evenings, however, it didn't work out because of my work schedule. As I continued to chart my time, I noticed that my only options were to either wake up earlier or go to bed later in order to spend time with God in praise and worship, prayer then reading the Bible. After discovering my time, according to my chart, I had to place God first by starting my day with Him. I decided to wake up earlier. I knew that no matter what, nothing could come between me having my time with God. Tired or not, I had to meet Him at the identified time.

When finding the time to spend with God, it will take the help of the Holy Spirit, our dedication and willpower (choice) to continue chasing God. As you find time in your schedule to spend with God, seek other ways to increase your time with Him. Limit your social media, phone time or TV time, for your continued growth in God. I believe you can do it!

Let's find some time in your schedule to spend with God

Step 1: Prayer

Father God,

Thank you for loving me unconditionally, my desire is to spend time with you and to include you in my day. I pray that you help me by the leading of your spirit to identify and or open up the specific time in my day in which you desire for us to have together for prayer and reading your word. In Jesus Name! Amen

Step 2: Gather Supplies: Paper, pencil & ruler

Step 3: Start charting your schedule on the paper

Below, I've listed an example chart for your review. As you review your personal schedule, find an available time and determine your length of time for prayer and study time. Once your time has been identified, strive to meet the Lord at that time every day, I'm certain He'll be expecting you.

6:00 a.m.	Normal Wake-up Time Morning Routine	Normal Wake-up Time Morning Routine	Normal Wake-up Time Morning Routine	Normal Wake-up Time Morning Routine	Normal Wake-up Time Morning Routine	Sleeping In	Sleeping In
7:00a.m.-7:30 a.m.	Open Time 30 minutes	Open Time 30 minutes	Open Time 30 minutes	Open Time 30 minutes	Open Time 30 minutes	Open Time 30 minutes	Open Time 30 minutes
8:00 a.m.-5:00 p.m.	Working	Working	Working	Working	Working	Free Time	Free Time
6:00 p.m.-8:00 p.m.	Arrival Home Dinner Nightly Routine	Arrival Home Dinner Nightly Routine	Arrival Home Dinner Nightly Routine	Arrival Home Dinner Nightly Routine	Arrival Home Dinner Nightly Routine	Free Time	Free Time
9:00 p.m.-10:00 p.m.	Open Time 1 hour Bedtime	Open Time 1 hour Bedtime	Open Time 1 hour Bedtime	Open Time 1 hour Bedtime	Open Time 1 hour Bedtime	Open Time 1 hour Bedtime	Open Time 1 hour Bedtime

Secret Place

~ Matthew 6:6 (NIV) ~

But when you pray, go into your room, close the door and pray to your Father, who is unseen. Then your Father, who sees what is done in secret, will reward you.

When I initially became a Christian, I was thirteen years of age. I really didn't understand much about Christianity during that time. However, I knew that I was born again because I had asked Jesus Christ to come into my heart. I was baptized, which showed my public outward confession by accepting Jesus into my heart, by faith. I went to church, served and participated in church events and, I thought, that was all to it. Until after I experienced my awakening, I learned that Christianity is a relationship with Jesus Christ.

As discussed earlier, I removed everything I was taught and went for it ya'll! As I began to pray, I didn't know what confessions and repentance was at that time, I didn't know about the different types of postures that the Bible speaks about when praying. I wasn't a Bible scholar. I literally sat down, crisscross apple sauce, on the floor and started to pray in a quiet, private place in my home, my closet. In my quite place it felt weird, initially, because I felt that no one was there or even listening. But that wasn't true. I soon realized that He was actually there; God promised us He was always with us and He would never leave or forsake us (Deuteronomy 31:6 (NIV). I realized that it wasn't complicated when starting to converse with God in prayer while in my closet, because through the Holy Spirits guidance, He led me into discovering the truth about me and Him. It was as if a flashlight was exposing the depths of my very soul and I wanted to open up and share willingly; there was a feeling of love in that closet. I prayed prior to my awakening, but this time, when I prayed, I experienced God in a completely different way, I encountered God's presence, which changed my life forever.

As I reflect upon my prayer life before receiving my awakening experience, I would usually pray in bed while lying down, or I would find myself praying to God in my mind or walking around praying underneath my breath. I'm not mentioning this to discredit prayer in any way. I believe all praying ways work. However, it was important for me to be consistent and to follow the pattern of Jesus by going to a place of solitude to be alone with God. Jesus, while on earth, would slip away from the disciples and crowds to spend alone time with Father God.

This place of solitude, the Bible refers to it as the secret place. It is a specific place of your choice with only you and God. This is a place where your spirit is quiet, all of the noisiness of day to day life is shut out, it is also a place of transparency, to connect with God on a more intimate level, regardless of the things that may be going on around us. When we spend time alone with God, He draws us closer and closer to Him and He begins to reveal Himself to us on a deeper level. God also reveals and exposes our hearts and inner motives and teaches us how to be more like Him. We began to take root in the fruit of the spirit by showing love, joy, peace, forbearance, kindness, faithfulness, goodness, gentleness and having self-control, Galatians 5:22-23 (NIV).

So, go for it in prayer, spending alone time with God. I encourage you to do something that you may not have done before. First, start off by praising God for what He has done, praise will place you in the presence of God; then it leads to worshipping God for who He is and ends in prayer in your secret place or your place of solitude. "Close the door and pray to your Father, who is unseen. Then your Father, who sees what is done in secret, will reward you. Matthew 6:6 (NIV)

Create your Secret Place

I encourage you to take some time this week to identify your secret place for you and God to meet and be alone away from everyone. It can be identified in your closet, your car, restroom, a corner chair, an office area, your bedroom, laundry room or any identifiable place of your choice. If in your home, you can make this area warm and cozy by bringing electrical candles, pillows or maybe even blankets. This is a place for you and Father God to be together in developing your individual relationship with Him. I'm so excited for you!

Studying the Bible

~ Matthew 4:4 (NIV) ~

Jesus answered, "It is written: 'Man shall not live on bread alone, but on every word that comes from the mouth of God.'

Spending time with God includes reading and studying God's word. As Christians, this means we have to open our Bibles to read and study the word of God, in order for us to be prosperous in whatever we do (Psalm 1:3 NIV). The Bible provides us with instructions for our life. According to 2 Timothy 3:16 (NLT), it teaches us what is true, makes us realize what is wrong in our lives, corrects us when we are wrong and teaches us to do what is right; helps us to grow in our relationship with God. It is as if we received a manual from a manufacturer on how to properly assemble a table. If we do not assemble the table correctly, according to the manual, our table can be improperly assembled, which can lead to us having a leaning and off track table. What I'm saying here is that God wants us to read and study His word because He loves us and it is His very words to us. When we face difficult circumstances and challenges in our lives, Gods word is there to give us direction, knowledge and wisdom to help us on our Christian journey. If we do not read and study His word, we can be improperly aligned not knowing Gods will for our lives. This can lead to frustration in all areas of our lives. We can also become lost without a sense of direction and purpose.

The Bible is also our protection from the enemy's attacks and his false representatives/teachers in the earth. This gives us one reason why we cannot depend on knowing and learning God and the Bible through others, we must know and grasp an understanding for ourselves. I can recall at one point in my life, I would repeat what others would say about a scripture not knowing if it was true or not. I would use it in the same phrase they did as if I knew it for myself, but guys, this wasn't a good thing. If you are like I was, start today by learning and reading the Bible for yourself or you could become easily deceived.

I encourage you to read and study the Bible and to not be discouraged when reading starting out. I'll share with you my story. When I initially began reading the Bible, I didn't understand its language, but I couldn't put the Bible down. So, I decided that I was not going to allow my feelings of not understanding to defeat me, I had to push through with a made up mind to overcome the obstacles that attempted to deflect me from reading and studying the Bible. I then began reading other translations to help with my understanding as the Holy Spirit was there to help me as well. I went to a Christian bookstore and one of the clerks showed me, that there were different Bible versions, parallel Bibles and commentary Bibles that I could reference when reading and studying, I had my new Bible engraved that day. After purchasing these helpful resources, I also used my phone's Bible app to refer to other translations for a better understanding.

As I would approach a word that was not very clear to me, I would search that words definition, in order to obtain a better understanding. In addition to that, I would refer to the words synonym to get a better breakdown for more clarity. I also found it helpful to journal by using the S.O.A.P method, which is a resource that I found on an internet source:

- S (scripture) - Identify a scripture from the Bible and write it out on a piece of paper.
- O (observation) - Read the scripture, what are the identifiable observations?
- A (application) - Based upon reading and studying the scripture, what can you apply in your daily life?
- P (prayer) - At the end of your studying the scripture, pray in response to God's word.

As I would approach a scripture, I would write it down and take it through the S.O.A.P. method. Eventually I found myself graduating from this method as I began to study the Bible more often. I noticed that it was becoming to be more and more interesting and fun because I could just read a few chapters and the Holy Spirit would give me revelation as to what the scripture or chapter referenced. Then I eventually increased my reading and studying time from 10 minutes to 30 minutes per day, before the start of my day. I also found it helpful to read when I would arrive at my place of employment or during my lunch break. I would read a daily devotional or scripture, either before my day started (depending upon my duties for that day) or I would either end my day with reading my daily devotional. Then as I began to end my day at home before resting, I would also read a scripture.

I found these methods to be helpful as a way to meditate on the word of God. In Psalm 1:2-3 (NIV), it states "but whose delight is in the law of the LORD, and who meditates on his law day and night. That person is like a tree planted by streams of water, which yields its fruit in the season and whose leaf does not wither- whatever they do prospers." By meditating on God's word it dwells in our hearts which is the inner core of who we really are. As the word enters into our hearts it begins to spill over to the life that we live and others will began to be impacted and inspired by Jesus Christ who lives within us. I encourage you to find ways that work best for you when reading and meditating on God's word day and night. 2 Timothy 2:15 (NIV) says, "Do your best to present yourself to God as one approved, a worker who does not need to be ashamed and who correctly handles the word of truth. This means we look to God for approval in our studying and not man. It requires us to be diligent and disciplined in our service to God, so that we can be confident in knowing and discerning between right and wrong.

If you haven't done so already, consider downloading a bible app and reference the different bible translations, in order to gather a better understanding of scripture. Also, consider purchasing your own tangible Bible. I believe, with the help of the Holy Spirit, by opening your Bible you're on your way to being Purpose Unstoppable!

~ Daily Bible Reading Challenge ~

When I began reading the Bible, I realized in order to read the Bible I had to become disciplined. My thoughts and flesh went against my willingness to sit down and read for a longer period of time. In order to become disciplined, I had to use my cell phone alarm as a timer. I set my timer for 10 minutes and I gradually shifted to reading 30 minutes per day.

Now, I would like to challenge you to start setting your cell phone alarm, or any alarm, when reading the Bible. Set it to a minimum of 10-15 minutes per day, for the next 30 days. After 30 days, gradually increase your reading to 20-30 minutes per day and beyond. I believe you can do it, don't feel stressed if you miss a day, just pick up where you left off and continue reading and studying daily.

Hearing God's Voice

~ John 10:27 (NIV) ~

My sheep listen to my voice; I know them, and they follow me.

I can recall the very first time ever hearing the Holy Spirit speak to me in the way that He did. It was shortly after experiencing my awakening. It was overwhelming; it was as if I was a clean pipe allowing me to clearly hear Him. After realizing what was occurring, I began to write down exactly what the Holy Spirit was saying. I received a message of specific instructions and I was given a glimpse of some of the plans God had for my life. After spending more time with God, we began to have longer conversations and I also became aware of the different ways in which He would speak to me other than hearing His voice. God is always speaking to us, when you cannot hear His voice. You can always hear the Holy Spirit speak in many different ways in which we as unique individuals can understand.

We can hear God speak to us;

Through the Bible: God will always speak to us through His word. 2 Timothy 3:16 -17(NLT) "All Scripture is inspired by God and is useful to teach us what is true and to make us realize what is wrong in our lives. It corrects us when we are wrong and teaches us to do what is right. God uses it to prepare and equip his people to do every good work."

> **My experience: There have been many times, I would read the Bible and I could not turn the page or read further because the Holy Spirit was speaking to me in that particular section of scripture.**

Through Other Believers: God uses people to speak to us. People can speak to us through music, TV programs, books, podcast, and sermons. God can also have strangers and Prophets speak to us as well. 2 Timothy 2:21 (NLT) says, "If you keep yourself pure, you will be a special utensil for honorable use. Your life will be clean, and you will be ready for the Master to use you for every good work."

> **My experience: The Holy Spirit instructed me to approach a woman and give her a hug, when I did the lady began crying. After receiving the hug, she said I needed that hug. I have also received prophetic messages from Prophets of the Lord informing and confirming things to come.**

Through Dreams and Visions: God uses dreams and visions to relay messages to us or for believers to give a message to others by interpretation. Joel 2:28 (NLT) "Then, after doing all those things, I will pour out my Spirit upon all people. Your sons and daughters will prophesy. Your old men will dream dreams, and your young men will see visions."

> **My experience: God allows me to operate in the seer realm. By the Holy Spirits leading He will instruct me to give a message to a person through either the dream or vision. He also speaks to me through the dreams that He gives to me personally.**

These are just a few of the most common ways God communicates to us other than hearing His voice directly. Therefore, we cannot place our Supernatural God in a box; He's just too big to fit in it. God knows exactly what we need to hear and when we need to hear from Him. He goes out of His way in order to convey a message to His children.

If you are having a hard time hearing God's voice, take into consideration the amount of time spent in the presence of God; in prayer, reading/studying the word of God and fasting. In addition to this, ask God to allow you to hear His voice. Matthew 7:7-8 (NIV) says "Ask and it will be given to you; seek and you will find; knock and the door will be opened to you. For everyone who asks receives; the one who seeks finds; and to the one who knocks, the door will be opened." Don't give up in the process!

~ Prayer ~

I encourage you to spend more time with God not only to hear His voice but because you want to know Him for who He is. Let us pray.

Father God,

Thank you for being who you are, my creator. I desire to know you more and more on a personal and intimate level. I draw close to you on today and I am so very grateful and thankful that you love me so very much to respond to me by drawing close to me. Lead me by your spirit on the path to knowing you more. My heart is open and willing. Show me the ways in which we can spend more time together throughout my day and show me the things I need to remove from my life so that I can hear you more clearly. There's more to the Christian life that I want to experience, I give you full permission to change my life. Fill me up with your spirit and take me to another level in you. In Jesus' Name Amen!

~ Chapter Scriptural Reflections ~

Developing My Relationship With God

"I am the vine; you are the branches. If you remain in me and I in you, you will bear much fruit; apart from me you can do nothing.

John 15:5 (NIV)

Finding Time to Spend with God

But seek first his kingdom and his righteousness, and all these things will be given to you as well.

Matthew 6:33 (NIV)

But the fruit of the Spirit is love, joy, peace, forbearance, kindness, goodness, faithfulness, gentleness and self-control. Against such things there is no law.

Galatians 5:22-23 (NIV)

Secret Place

But when you pray, go into your room, close the door and pray to your Father, who is unseen. Then your Father, who sees what is done in secret, will reward you.

Matthew 6:6 (NIV)

Be strong and courageous. Do not be afraid or terrified because of them, for the LORD your God goes with you; he will never leave you nor forsake you."

Deuteronomy 31:6 (NIV)

But the fruit of the Spirit is love, joy, peace, forbearance, kindness, goodness, faithfulness, gentleness and self-control. Against such things there is no law.

Galatians 5:22-23 (NIV)

Studying the Bible

Jesus answered, "It is written: 'Man shall not live on bread alone, but on every word that comes from the mouth of God.'

Matthew 4:4 (NIV)

It states "but whose delight is in the law of the LORD, and who meditates on his law day and night. That person is like a tree planted by streams of water, which yields its fruit in the season and whose leaf does not wither- whatever they do prosper."

Psalm 1:2-3 (NIV)

All scripture is inspired by God and is useful to teach us what is true and to make us realize what is wrong in our lives. It corrects us when we are wrong and teaches us to do what is right.

2 Timothy 3:16 (NLT)

Do your best to present yourself to God as one approved, a worker who does not need to be ashamed and who correctly handles the word of truth.

2 Timothy 2:15 (NIV)

Hearing God's Voice

My sheep listen to my voice; I know them, and they follow me.

John 10:27 (NIV)

All Scripture is inspired by God and is useful to teach us what is true and to make us realize what is wrong in our lives. It corrects us when we are wrong and teaches us to do what is right. God uses it to prepare and equip his people to do every good work.

2 Timothy 3:16-17 (NLT)

If you keep yourself pure, you will be a special utensil for honorable use. Your life will be clean, and you will be ready for the Master to use you for every good work.

2 Timothy 2:21 (NLT)

"Then, after doing all those things, I will pour out my spirit upon all people. Your sons and daughters will prophesy. Your old men will dream dreams and your young men will see visions."

Joel 2:28 (NLT)

"Ask and it will be given to you; seek and you will find; knock and the door will be opened to you. For everyone who asks receives; the one who seeks finds; and to the one who knocks, the door will be opened.

Matthew 7:7-8 (NIV)

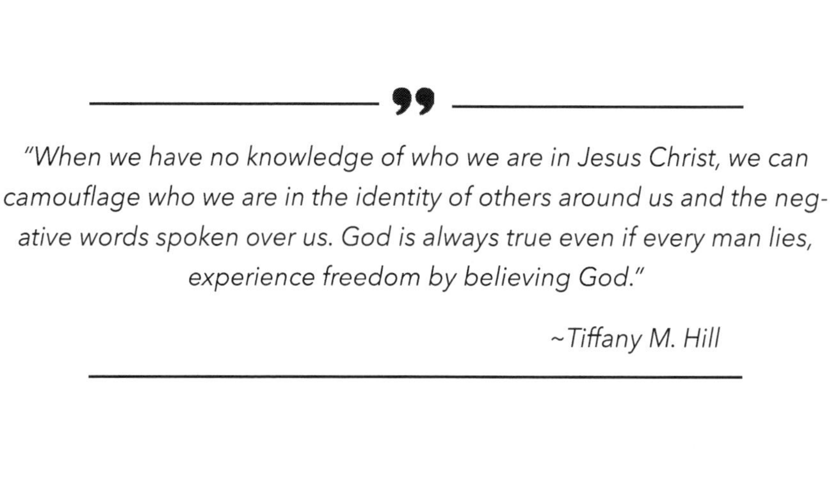

"When we have no knowledge of who we are in Jesus Christ, we can camouflage who we are in the identity of others around us and the negative words spoken over us. God is always true even if every man lies, experience freedom by believing God."

~Tiffany M. Hill

2

Knowing Who You Are

~ 1 Peter 2:9-10 (NLT) ~

"But you are not like that, for you are a chosen people. You are royal priests, a holy nation, and God's very own possession. As a result, you can show others the goodness of God, for he called you out of the darkness into his wonderful light. Once you had no identity as a people; now you are God's people. Once you received no mercy; now you have received God's mercy"

I suffered with low self-esteem and insecurity by having negative words spoken over my life. I was told I was too dark and that I was not smart enough. I looked to others to define my identity and I tried finding it in mentors, degrees and in my professional career, and that was unsuccessful. You may have experienced this or something similar to my experience. Often times, without knowing any better, we believed the lies from the pit of hell, without considering what God our creator has to say about who we are. God is always true even when every man lies, so believe God and not man. As I continued walking with the Lord, this is when I received revelation that we cannot know who we are apart from Jesus Christ. As believers, God intends for us to find our identity in Him.

Our identity is not based upon a professional career title, race, ethnicity, what we see on television or social media or even our relationships. It is also not based upon the negative words that others may have used to define who they thought we were to them. But as believers by faith, our identity is in Jesus Christ. 1 Peter 2:9-10 (NLT) is one of many scriptures that tell us who we are; I believe this scripture will help in identifying your true identity as it did for me. It reads,

"But you are not like that, for you are a chosen people. You are royal priests, a holy nation, and God's very own possession. As a result, you can show others the goodness of God, for he called you out of the darkness into his wonderful light. Once you had no identity as a people; now you are God's people. Once you received no mercy; now you have received God's mercy"

Remember we are:

Chosen - we are chosen by God and that means we are not an accident. Our parents might have been surprised by the pregnancy, but God wasn't surprised. You were planned by God. So much so that he created you before he created the world. Before we were conceived in our mother's womb, God made all the delicate, inner parts of our bodies and formed us in our mother's womb. He knows exactly who you are because you come from Him. He knows exactly why He sent you on earth at this appointed time. You were supposed to be born when you were born and you are supposed to be living and breathing today. Know that you're not an accident; you are selected by God as His ambassador, making His appeal through you, to call His people back to Him through your particular assignment.

A Royal Priest - as Christians, we are Kingdom citizens and that means we have special privileges and access to His promises. We are also representatives on earth from heaven and our role is to teach others about where we come from through God's word.

Holy Nation - we are set apart by God for good works to serve Him.

And that means, as believers, we cannot do what everyone else is doing if it is not of God.

God's Special Possession - we belong to Almighty God. We are a people of His own special creation. He didn't choose the planets, animals, Angels or any other creation to be His special possession, but we are. He found us worthy enough to send His son Jesus Christ to die for our sins, to redeem us from suffering death and in that we are the purchased possessions who are to glorify Him.

*Received God's Mercy - God being mer*ciful means that when we deserve punishment, He doesn't punish us. In fact He blesses us instead. Mercy is the withholding of a just condemnation when we deserve punishment; the Lord rewards us instead. For instance, if we were to go before a judge because we ran a traffic light, we know that we are guilty. We cannot pay the fine or serve time; the judge shows us mercy by sending us out of the door without punishment. Hallelujah! Now knowing who you are, refuse to believe and accept negative words spoken over your life that do not align with the word of God. Think of yourself the way God thinks of you. God loves you and wants you to be free and not bound.

~ Speak over yourself ~

I believe it is important to speak positive statements that can help you know what God says about you and how special you are to Jesus Christ. Develop a new habit by repeating I am statements daily to encourage yourself while on your journey.

- I am a child of God, John 1:12 (NIV) Yet to all who did receive him, to those who believed in his name, he gave the right to become children of God.
- I am created in God's image, Genesis 1:27 (NIV) So God created mankind in his own image, in the image of God he created them; male and female he created them.
- I am fearfully and wonderfully made, Psalm 139:14 (NIV) I praise you because I am fearfully and wonderfully made; your works are wonderful, I know that full well.
- *I am loved by God, John 3:16 (NLT)* "For this is how God loved the world: He gave his one and only Son, so that everyone who believes in him will not perish but have eternal life.

Insert your own positive statement and scripture here.

Try this: Write your I am statements on a mirror in your home. I often write encouraging words on my bathroom mirror with a dry erase marker and I recite them in the mornings and at the end of my day.

Going in Circles

~ 1 Corinthians 14:33 (NKJV) ~

For God is not the author of confusion but of peace, as in all the churches of the saints.

Before experiencing my awakening, I would often feel an indescribable pull from within. It was a pull of wanting a change and realizing that my life was not designed or created to be without purpose; a knowing of what I was created to do and who I really was. This pulling feeling never went away. I would often hear others say, "Your passion is your purpose." But I was truly the person saying "well, I'm not exactly sure what my passion is or my purpose." I was confused, going in circles. I can recall preparing for college, not knowing what to choose for a major. I went from being interested in three different degree programs and landed in the field of Social Work because I was just confused ya'll. As I continued through the process of completing my degree program, after my internship, I commented to my professor..." I really don't want to major in Social Work anymore." I would look at other people around me and wonder why they were as passionate, confident and certain about what they were to do with their lives and I wasn't. I thought maybe, once I graduated and began working, my passion and purpose would reveal itself, but it wasn't revealed until I began developing my personal relationship with God.

When dealing with confusion, I couldn't make a decision about a major or career and I didn't know then that God created me for a certain plan that only I could fulfill. I thought that the routine of life without purpose: going to work, paying your bills, wash and repeat, was the way of life. That turned out to be very frustrating and untruthful. Confusion of your mind is one of many tactics that the enemy uses to attack your identity in order for you not to determine who you really are in Jesus Christ and to also prevent you from identifying your purpose. The enemy feeds us lies to get us off course. The enemy lied and used confusion as a tactic on me by keeping me going in circles.

Refuse to be confused. God will provide you with peace and direction; He is not the author of confusion. God wants us to lean on Him for everything. When we are leaning on our own understanding this brings about confusion. We were not created to live apart from God. When we seek God's will for our lives, He will show us the path to take. Proverbs 3:5-6 (NLT) says, "Trust in the LORD with all your heart; do not depend on your own understanding. Seek his will in all you do, and he will show you which path to take."

I Am Good Enough

~ Ephesians 2:10 (NLT) ~

For we are God's masterpiece. He has created us anew in Christ Jesus, so we can do the good things he planned for us long ago.

The feeling of not good enough is a feeling you may have felt sometime in your life, whether it was in school, amongst your family and friends or in a job. For me, there was a time in my life when I struggled in this area of feeling that I wasn't good enough. I believe this was one reason that encouraged me in being the person God called me to be. I thought I was insignificant because of my experiences or challenges I faced. I never seemed to fit in with the crowd as a child or even in young adulthood, I felt uncomfortable in most environments around some friends and family and I always tried to find my place to belong.

I wasn't the highest performing student in school when it came to my academics or the best at any sport, I've ever played. I always had the determination and drive within to want to be the best me that I could be. It was something on the inside of me telling me that I was someone special. I could remember, always wanting to be the person called to receive an award at school programs or to be inducted into the National Honor Society. The society members would walk around the auditorium and surprise the new inductees by tapping the individuals on their shoulders to drape them with a yellow cord in receipt of this great honor. I often tried to make the better grades, not to compete with anyone, but to fill the void from within, of how do I belong and am I good enough. The awards I would receive were more like.... thanks for attending and graduating! And this often left me feeling overlooked.

Here's the thing, God accepts you and wants you just as you are. School awards and where you come from do not determine what you are capable of as a believer in Jesus Christ. Ephesians 2:10 (NLT) states "we are God's masterpiece. He has created us anew in Christ Jesus, so we can do the good things he planned for us long ago. As His masterpiece you are God's work of art, He designed and created your personality, beauty and desires of your heart specifically for His purpose and glory. You may have felt you wanted to change something about yourself, but God thinks you're great just the way that you are. Walk in confidence knowing that God can use everything you think He cannot use. Your challenges, choices and experiences come with you along the way on your purposeful journey to inspire, motivate and to encourage others that if you can get through they can also.

~ Prayer ~

Father God,

I adore and honor you, there's no one else like you! I thank you that my identity is found in you and not in the world or what others have spoken over my life. I am your child and I am made in your image. What matters is who you say that I am. I refuse to be confused and I command the enemy to get underneath my feet. I trust you Lord with all of my heart and I lean to you for direction, peace and purpose. In Jesus' Name Amen!

~ Chapter Scriptural Reflections ~

Knowing Who You Are

"But you are not like that, for you are a chosen people. You are royal priests, a holy nation, and God's very own possession. As a result, you can show others the goodness of God, for he called you out of the darkness into his wonderful light. Once you had no identity as a people; now you are God's people. Once you received no mercy; now you have received God's mercy"

1 Peter 2:9-10 (NLT)

Yet all who did receive him, to those who believed in his name, he gave the right to become children of God.

John 1:12 (NIV)

So God created mankind in his own image, in the image of God he created them, male and female he created them.

Genesis 1:27 (NIV)

I praise you because I am fearfully and wonderfully made; your works are wonderful, I know that full well.

Psalm 139:14(NIV)

"For this is how God loved the world: He gave his one and only Son, so that everyone who believes in him will not perish but have eternal life.

John 3:16 (NLT)

Going in Circles

For God is not the author of confusion but of peace,
as in all the churches of the saints.

1 Corinthians 14:33 (NKJV)

Trust in the LORD with all your heart; do not depend on your own understanding. Seek his will in all you do, and he will show you which path to take.

Proverbs 3:5-6 (NLT)

I Am Good Enough

For we are God's masterpiece. He has created us anew in Christ Jesus, so we can do the good things he planned for us long ago.

Ephesians 2:10 (NLT)

"God is not condemning us, He's forgiven us. Don't be ashamed of your past; shake it off, because it's covered under the blood of Jesus!"

~Tiffany M. Hill

3

Deliverance From the Past

~ Romans 8:1 (NLT) ~

So now there is no condemnation for those who belong to Christ Jesus.

On my continued walk with the Lord after my awakening, the Lord set me free from depression and the shamefulness of my past. I was faced with an unplanned pregnancy at the age of sixteen. In the midst of my active, athletic high school accomplishments, everything came to a screeching halt. I couldn't believe it; I played basketball and was also a majorette. I thought, what was I going to do now? As expected, my family didn't take the news very well at all. But how could I blame them? My Mother hyperventilated in a brown paper bag. I'm a Daddy's girl, so it hurt me just to see his face; both my parents believed in me. My sisters cried, they couldn't believe it either. I was their role model and my brother, who was away in school during that time, was crushed. After the shock of it all, the experience led me to feel ashamed. I felt that I had disappointed everyone who loved and cared for me, especially my family and my younger sisters. Each day I would look at my younger sisters who looked up to me, with the thought of "I'm sorry I let you down."

Although, I knew I was loved and supported, no one really understood my real pain and as a result it led me deep down into the dark hole of depression and I began to punish myself. I felt that I no longer deserved to enjoy life around me, therefore I would keep myself isolated and I would refuse to attend fun and enjoyable events. But as the depression increased, I became numb on the inside and I found myself simply going through the motions of life. Throughout it all, I still attended school regularly, squeezing out a smile in hopes to feel some form of joy. I was shunned by a few teachers and friends at school. I can recall one of my friends who looked up to me, stating that her parents no longer wanted her to interact with me because of my pregnancy. I respected her parents' wishes and we never spoke from that moment forward. I didn't know what I was getting myself into, I knew I made a decision that would impact my life forever and it wasn't intentional to harm or hurt anyone.

I made a bold decision to keep my baby and I did not consider abortion even though the option was brought to my attention. I made the right decision, despite the fear, the shame and the opposition I faced. I delivered a beautiful, healthy baby girl, and I graduated from high school-having the support of my family. I didn't want them to be burdened with my responsibility but they hung in there with me every step of the way and encouraged me to be the best mother I knew to be. My family also supported me as I continued to further my education, pursuing my undergraduate degree. I understood that this was not the time to give up; it was a time to be responsible and grow into maturation. Fast forward seventeen years later; my beautiful daughter continues to be an exceptional child. She's been an honor roll student since the start of elementary school and now in high school and I couldn't be more proud.

At times, we can become discouraged or disappointed from the choices we've made. We can also feel left out, overlooked and judged from past experiences but the good news is that, there's no condemnation for those who belong to Christ Jesus says Romans 8:1 (NLT). God is not mad at you; He's madly in love with you. When you have accepted Jesus Christ as your Lord and savior everything that you ever did is erased by the blood of Jesus. It is as if you committed a crime and your fingerprints are left all over the crime scene, and Jesus' blood covers your fingerprints as if you were never there. Therefore, you no longer accept those feelings of disappointment, shamefulness and discouragement from your past, because it doesn't align with Jesus' work on the cross. Do not accept others reminding you of what you've done. Your past definitely doesn't define you, but it makes you stronger and it connects us to God for Him to be able to grow and develop you in Him from every experience for the journey ahead. Remember that God's grace is all you need, His power works best in weakness, for when you are weak, then you are strong, 2 Corinthians 12:9-11 (NIV).

Release It

~ 1 John 1:9 (NIV) ~

If we confess our sins, he is faithful and just and will forgive us our sins and purify us from all unrighteousness.

Before my awakening experience, I did not have an understanding or knowledge of how to release what did not belong to me over to Jesus Christ through confessing my sins, asking God for forgiveness or even repentance. I walked around in life holding on to my past within, not having a clear understanding that Jesus had already paid the price for my sins by His blood. But by the leading of the Holy Spirit while in His presence, He led me first to confess my sins, I then asked Him for forgiveness and repentance of my sins soon followed. In 1 John 1:9 (NIV) it states "if we confess our sins, he is faithful and just and will forgive us our sins and purify us from all unrighteousness." I can recall once I made my confession of the sins I committed, the release of it was such a blessing. I felt as if a load was being lifted during the entire process. It was as if a light shined upon me to expose what was in darkness; as the Holy Spirit began to bring back memories of the things of my past that I thought I'd forgotten. I couldn't believe how far back the Holy Spirit lead me to confess the things of my past. As the thoughts began coming to mind, I would immediately confess my sins out loud as an overflow of tears ran profusely down my face with a remorseful heart towards the Lord. I then asked for forgiveness and I repented of the things I confessed that was not pleasing to Him. When I repented it was as if a brick wall was raised. I was unable to go back living the way I lived prior to meeting God. During this experience the Lord did not make me feel ashamed but rather, I felt His love cover me completely.

If you've made choices that were not pleasing to the Lord, and you're still holding on to what Jesus has already covered with His blood God wants you to release it. He doesn't want you to conceal your sin; He wants you to be prosperous. Therefore, decide today to release it all and, in your private time with the Lord, don't feel ashamed because the Lord helps you (Isaiah 50:7 NIV). He wants you to draw near to Him.

By repenting of your sins, it means "to realize that the kind of life we are living is wrong and that we must adopt a completely new set of values." To that end, according to William Barclay, it involves two things. It involves sorrow for what we have been and it involves the resolve that by the grace of God we will be changed. When we repent we change our mind and we turn away from sin and turn towards doing the will of God. We receive forgiveness for our sins by our Lord and savior Jesus Christ's death and resurrection. This means the sins you have committed, He wipes away on your behalf and He remembers them no more, Hebrews 8:12 (ESV); that's Amazing! Thank you Lord. You don't ever have to feel guilty or ashamed of the choices you made from your past, or from something you may have done currently or what someone has done to hurt you. Release that heavy load because Jesus carries this for you. Give the Lord permission to invade your space to set you free from the bondage of sin, guilt and shamefulness.

God wants His children to be free and I believe we receive this freedom when

We begin to develop our personal relationship with God. Our lives begin changing when we start with God, and by His spirit He guides us into all truths. I did not realize the condition I was in as living a sinful life until I was drawn back to God. He began to reveal to me the things that were not pleasing to Him. I thought I was living a normal life but in reality my life was without God in all areas.

Renewing our minds. The Lord began revealing to me the scriptures that related to my condition and transformation began taking root as I started to apply the word to my life. We have a renewed mind by being doers and not only hearers of the word, deceiving ourselves, James 1:22(ESV). Our minds are not renewed because we know the word of God in and out. It changes through making an effort to apply the word to our lives and this is when it becomes flesh, displaying in our actions and thoughts transforming us from the inside out.

Share your testimony with others. When I began talking to others about my shame of being a teenage mother, I noticed I felt better. Prior, I had no desire to share my story or my age with others because I felt they would judge me. James 5:16 (NIV) says, "Therefore confess your sins to each other and pray for each other so that you may be healed. The prayer of a righteous person is powerful and effective." I believe there is healing in our confessing, sharing with others our faults as a living testimony.

Casting down negative thoughts. The enemy tells us the opposite of who we really are in Jesus Christ, when he condemns us in our thoughts. Talk back to the enemy by using scripture or positive words of encouragement to replace what does not align with who God says you are. 2 Corinthians 10:5 (NLT) says, "We destroy every proud obstacle that keeps people from knowing God. We capture their rebellious thoughts and teach them to obey Christ."

Accept and receive your forgiveness. Refuse to feel bad about yourself every day. When you have asked God for forgiveness you are forgiven. Here's a rule: Give yourself two days to mope around and on the third day walk in your forgiveness. We are not perfect, we take our flaws to God and He helps us in our weaknesses.

Through it all, the great benefits of the process leads to a more intimate and deeper relationship with the Lord Jesus Christ our Savior, who truly loves us more than we could ever imagine. In sharing my story throughout this chapter, I've learned to rise above the difficult situations and the choices I made, by allowing Jesus Christ to show up through me by making a choice to follow Him. With this, God restored feelings of shamefulness and depression from my past and in my private time with the Lord, He shared with me that I wasn't insignificant to Him and that I meant so much more to Him, than I had ever thought. He loves us in spite of our choices and He will continue to see us through. If God delivered, restored and uplifted me, He will absolutely do the same thing for you. The pain of our past, I believe, is not meant to be forgotten, but rather it is intended for God to use it for His glory. It allows us to share our experiences in order for us to share how He delivered, redeemed and restored us to others as living, breathing and walking testimonies. So, do not feel ashamed, disappointed or discouraged, God loves you! Our choices and experiences allow for better choices in the future.

~ Make a Declaration ~

Before making your declaration, stand up with confidence speaking forth the declaration believing that you have received it and it will be yours.

"I will not allow my past to keep me in bondage and ashamed, because it is covered under the blood of my Lord and Savior Jesus Christ. I am not looking backwards; I am growing in God, looking ahead for what God has for me, I am not insignificant, I have purpose and God loves me." In Jesus' name, Amen.

~ Chapter Scriptural Reflections ~

Deliverance From the Past

So now there is no condemnation for those who belong to Christ Jesus.

Romans 8:1 (NLT)

But he said to me, "My grace is sufficient for you, for my power is made perfect in weakness." Therefore I will boast all the more gladly about my weaknesses, so that Christ's power may rest on me. **10** *That is why, for Christ's sake, I delight in weaknesses, in insults, in hardships, in persecutions, in difficulties. For when I am weak, then I am strong.*

2 Corinthians 12:9-11 (NIV)

Release It

If we confess our sins, he is faithful and just and will forgive us our sins and purify us from all unrighteousness.

1 John 1:9 (NIV)

Because the Sovereign LORD helps me, I will not be disgraced. Therefore have I set my face like flint, and I know I will not be put to shame.

Isaiah 50:7 (NIV)

For I will be merciful toward their iniquities, and I will remember their sins no more."

Hebrews 8:12 (ESV)

But be doers of the word, and not hearers only, deceiving yourselves.

James 1:22 (ESV)

Therefore confess your sins to each other and pray for each other so that you may be healed. The prayer of a righteous person is powerful and effective.

James 5:16 (NIV)

We destroy every proud obstacle that keeps people from knowing God. We capture their rebellious thoughts and teach them to obey Christ"

2 Corinthians 10:5 (NLT)

"We may all arrive at our destination differently, some may travel by plane, train or car, but what matters is that we all get there bringing Glory to God."

~Tiffany M. Hill

4

God's Plan for Your Life

~ Jeremiah 29:11 (NIV) ~

For I know the plans I have for you," declares the LORD, "plans to prosper you and not to harm you, plans to give you hope and a future.

I could hear Gods voice very clearly as He spoke to me and called me to do His work; this was shortly after having my awakening experience. He said to me, "your calling is a high calling, its Ministry, minster to my people and tell them what I tell you to tell them." After receiving this prophecy, to be transparent, I really didn't quite grasp and understand what God said; I wasn't expecting to serve in that capacity. I really thought that was for other people, not me. My plan was to continue working as I was, in the field of Social Work. I never imagined that God had a plan already assigned for my life. I was thinking that whatever I thought and wanted to become, that's what I was to do in life. But when He revealed my calling, I truly wasn't looking for that, because I just wanted Him. I was having fun chasing after God and learning about Him and hearing other people's experiences and testimonies as to what He had done for them. I wanted to be in His presence and get my life together so that I could be pleasing to Him and to represent Him well. That's all I wanted.

However, as I continued to spend increasingly more time with God, it became clearer. He then began confirming, in our private time together, that I was to minister (serve) and to preach the gospel to His people. I accepted my calling and I realized that it fulfilled the void of having a place to belong. God created something specifically for me to do; it was one of my reasons for being here on earth at this appointed time. It was what I had longed and searched for, and I found it in truly searching for our Lord and Savior Jesus Christ. It was completely unexpected when God revealed the calling for my life. When He did, I noticed that my choices in life became much easier. I no longer had all the broad options of choosing the direction to go, as it related to job opportunities or a career change. I had what you would call tunnel vision. I knew what and who to entertain; it was easier choosing books to read. My focus was aligned and much clearer.

I would even experience that same focus as I would awake each morning, I would get up looking forward to fulfilling something that was greater than myself. It was important to me that God had given me something to do for Him and I did not want to let Him down. When we have no direction in our lives and we wake up to the routine of life and have nothing bigger than ourselves to fulfill. We tend to look at others around us and began competing with them because of the need for direction and true purpose. We also let others influence us as to the direction for our lives, even when it is the opposite of what God wants for us.

God wants us to accept the calling on our lives to fulfill our purpose, which is to glorify Him. If we do not accept our calling we cannot fulfill our purpose and our commitment to other Christians by building up the body of Christ and edifying the church. We are called the body of Christ for a reason; 1 Corinthians 12:12 (NLT) says "the human body has many parts, but the many parts make up one whole body. So it is with the body of Christ." This means each member of the body is a specific body part, we need one another to function properly as one whole body in doing the will of God. Our calling is an assignment given by God in order for us to fulfill our purpose. Our calling is our mode of transportation to get to our purpose, while using our gifts. Everyone's modes of transportation/gifts are different because we are all unique individuals, created to do a specific thing that only we can do. I'll share with you this analogy; if I created your cell phone and it doesn't properly work, then it is not doing the job that it was designed and created to do. We all bring glory to God when what He created functions in the way in which He designed us to function. This means you were born to meet a need, to make a difference, and to fulfill your purpose and leave this earth empty. You were not created to just go to work, pay your bills, go home and do it all over again. Because that's settling into the routine of life; this doesn't allow you to discover your greatest potential. It leads you to having no awareness to what you are placed here on earth to do in order to impact the world with what has been placed on the inside of you.

Ephesians 1:4(NLT) says, "Even before he made the world, God loved us and chose us in Christ to be holy and without fault in his eyes." The word holy in Greek is hagios, which means set apart and sacred. God told Jeremiah 1:5 (NIV), "Before I formed you in the womb, I knew you, and before you were born I set you apart; I appointed you as a prophet to the nations." These scriptures tells us that we are set apart for a task, a particular purpose, that only you were placed on earth to do for the Kingdom of God. If God revealed Jeremiahs plan for his life, He will certainly reveal His plan for your life. That means, from my experience, you have to be connected to God in prayer. This is where your relationship is birthed in order to hear clearly what God is saying to you. Go after God and seek Him with all your heart, not only for your calling but to develop your personal relationship with Him and everything else will be added.

~ Understanding Your Gifts ~

Understanding our gifts helps us determine the work God has called us to do for the body of Christ. These gifts have been given to believers for the building and strengthening of the body of Christ and to glorify God. Our gifts are without repentance. This means the gifts that God has given to you, He does not take back. Your gifts are in your possession to serve others and are not to be kept to yourself. The three categories of gifts have been listed below, in order to give a brief overview of our supernatural gifts for understanding.

Motivational Gifts

~ Romans 12:6-8 (NLT) ~

"In his grace, God has given us different gifts for doing certain things well. So if God has given you the ability to prophesy, speak out with as much faith as God has given you. If your gift is serving others, serve them well. If you are a teacher, teach well. If your gift is to encourage others, be encouraging. If it is giving, give generously. If God has given you leadership ability, take the responsibility seriously. And if you have a gift for showing kindness to others, do it gladly."

- *Prophecy*: also can be referred to as simple prophecy. In Greek, prophecy means a speaking forth. This gift does not foretell the future. But, it strengthens comforts and encourages others. There are many layers to prophecy.

- *Serving*: gift of servitude, loves to serve others, they keep the body of Christ moving.

- *Teacher*: researches and communicates complicated truths, they keep the body of Christ studying and learning the word of God.

- *Exhorter*: enjoys encouraging others, they are very positive; they counsel others and helps the body of Christ to apply spiritual truths.

- *Givers*: love to give money, time, talent and energy in order to meet needs, give without regrets.
- *Administrators*: organizes, leads, directs, and facilitates, to show the body of Christ how to increase in our vision.
- *Mercy*: shows compassion and provides personal and emotional support love and care to those in need. Immune to error.

Manifestation Gifts

~ 1 Corinthians 12:7-10 (NLT) ~

"A spiritual gift is given to each of us so we can help each other. To one person the Spirit gives the ability to give wise advice; to another the same Spirit gives a message of special knowledge. The same Spirit gives great faith to another, and to someone else the one Spirit gives the gift of healing. He gives one person the power to perform miracles, and another the ability to prophesy. He gives someone else the ability to discern whether a message is from the Spirit of God or from another spirit. Still another person is given the ability to speak in unknown languages, while another is given the ability to interpret what is being said."

The Inspirational/Vocal Gifts/Speaking Gifts - (these gifts say something).

- *Divers Kinds of tongues*: divers means more than one. There are two different types of operations for this supernatural gift and it is used for our heavenly prayer language and also as a sign to the unbeliever. When we are praying in our heavenly prayer language it edifies and uplifts us spiritually. We are also speaking directly to God. When we do not know what to pray, the spirit prays for us.
- Interpretation of Tongues: this supernatural gift can be interpreted in two different ways. For a person praying in their heavenly prayer language and also for a person speaking in an unknown

tongue to an individual or group.

- Prophecy: this supernatural gift also can be referred to as simple prophecy. In Greek prophecy means a speaking forth. This gift does not foretell the future. But, it strengthens comforts and encourages others. Note: There are many layers to the gift of prophecy.

The Revelatory Gifts - The revelatory gifts reveals something hidden, unknown or unrevealed - (these gifts reveal something).

- *Word of Knowledge*: this gift receives supernatural revelation from God of any facts. This can be about events, locations, names, specific information that we wouldn't know about otherwise.
- *Word of Wisdom*: this gift receives supernatural revelation from the mind of God about future events that have not occurred.
- *Discerning of Spirits*: this gift is not discernment. It is discerning of spirits. The Greek word for discerning is "diakrisis", which means to distinguish or judge something to see if it is evil or from God. It is the supernatural revelation to discern the present spirit that is in operation or active. Discerning of evil spirits or Godly spirits. With this gift our spiritual senses are opened up. We can see in the spirit, smell, taste, hear and touch in the spirit realm.

The Power Gifts - The power gifts express and manifest the power of God. It is power in action - (these gifts do something).

- *Gift of Faith or Special Faith*: this gift is the supernatural power given by God to receive a miracle. This gift is unshakable confidence in God, His word and promise. There's no doubt and no fear. This gift also comes and goes.
- *Gifts of Healing*: notice this is the only gift in the plural tense. It is the supernatural power given by God removing all diseases and infirmities. Healing all areas of the physical, mental, addictions

etc.

- *Working of Miracles*: supernatural power given by God to produce miracles beyond our natural comprehension.

Ministry Gifts

~ Ephesians 4:11-13 (NIV) ~

So Christ himself gave the apostles, the prophets, the evangelists, the pastors and teachers, to equip his people for works of service, so that the body of Christ may be built up until we all reach unity in the faith and in the knowledge of the Son of God and become mature, attaining to the whole measure of the fullness of Christ.

- *Apostle*: (to govern) An apostle is a sent one, a forerunner leading the charge and establishes churches.
- *Prophet*: (to guide) A prophet is a spokesperson for God. The prophet admonishes, warns, directs, encourages, intercedes, teaches and counsels. They bring the word of God to the people of God and lead the people back to God.
- *Evangelist*: (to gather) The Evangelist reaches the lost and proclaims the good news of the gospel of Jesus Christ.
- *Pastor*: (to guard) The primary terms that describe the role of the pastor are "elder," "bishop," and "teacher" (1 Timothy 3:1-13). "Elder," or episkopos (from which we get our word episcopal) refers to the oversight of the believers, and it involves teaching, preaching, caring, and exercising authority where needed. (Referenced from gotquestions.com) 1 Peter 5:2-4 (NIV) refers to the role of a Pastor it states, "Be Sheppard's of God's flock that is under your care, watching over them - not because you must, but because you are willing, as God wants you to be; not pursuing dishonest gain, but eager to serve; not lording it over those entrusted to you, but being examples to the flock."

- *Teacher*: (to garner) Researches and communicates complicated truths, they keep the body of Christ studying and learning the word of God. They are able to break down complex information to make it simple.

Persistency

~ Matthew 7:7 (NLT) ~

Keep on asking, and you will receive what you ask for. Keep on seeking, and you will find. Keep on knocking, and the door will be opened to you.

I recall having a conversation with one of my daughters about purpose, as we were discussing seeking God for her calling. As the conversation proceeded, we began role playing. I gave this example; if you wanted to find your cell phone, to what extreme would you go to in order to recover your cell phone, legally? And of course her response was very extreme, because her cell phone is near and dear to her heart, LOL! She wanted to break my car windows when one of the final scenarios was that her cell phone was probably locked in the car along with the keys to the vehicle. Although it was a fun exercise, I believe it is important for us to evaluate our persistency in pushing through in prayer.

Matthew 7:7 (NLT) states "Keep on asking, and you will receive what you ask for. Keep on seeking, and you will find. Keep on knocking, and the door will be opened to you." I believe this scripture has given us three levels of prayer. Starting with the first level which is asking, we can't just stop there with only asking God for the calling on our life and not go any further. We must push through to the next levels in prayer which is seeking and knocking. If we do not first ask then our request cannot be acknowledged. If we do not seek then we will not find what we are asking for and the door will not open to the person who chooses not to knock. This is not to rush God on a response. However, this scripture focuses on us having to be persistent in prayer; praying with a sincere heart for God to provide a response as to your calling.

I encourage you not to give up in prayer, continue pressing through. I have a few questions for you. How bad do you want to know why you were created? What should you truly be doing? Your purpose depends on your answer to these questions. God wants you to know and He wouldn't keep it from you. He knows what we need, our desires and feelings and especially what's best for us. God would not tell us, through His word, to pray and refuse to hear our prayers. Therefore, pray in faith with expectancy, and believe that you have received it, and it will be yours (Mark 11:24, NIV).

It's Time to Make Your Move

~ Jeremiah 29:13 (NIV) ~

You will seek me and find me when you seek me with all your heart.

I dreaded Monday's because it meant that I had to go to work. Conversely, I would jump for joy on Friday's because I was ready to be out of there. I was experiencing frustration; I wanted more out of life than what I was getting. The cycle of frustration, of not knowing what I was created to do, continued day by day and year after year. As I continued developing my relationship with God, I realized the reason why I was so frustrated. It was because I had no clue to the fact that I really didn't fully fit, something was missing. I felt as if I wasn't positioned or aligned completely on the path of my true purpose in life. I believe I fit partially, because there was a reason for God to have placed me in certain environments, but there was always something missing. I can remember trying to figure it all out on my own, without God, as to my reason for being created. I would answer questions when picking up magazines at the local store about what I was supposed to be doing in life and that all led me to a dead end, with no results. It all screamed frustration!

Once God revealed what I was supposed to be doing, the frustration slightly calmed down. I no longer focused on the job completing me; I knew there was something more for me to do. I understood that what I was called to do was not for me but it was for God to be glorified. Until you find out from God what you are supposed be doing on earth at this time now, you will continue to be frustrated, going from job to job or dreading Monday's. It's like this, if you were trying to put a piece of furniture together that you purchased, and it came with screws, if you tried to place the screw where it doesn't belong then your piece of furniture will not work properly. This means, in everything you do there will always be something missing.

It's time to make your move, if you're experiencing frustration, you don't know which way to turn, God is saying He has the answer and He knows everything! When you seek Him with all your heart you will find Him, Jeremiah 29:13 (NLT). He wants you to come to Him. Stop talking to everyone else and focus on Jesus. We can't expect God to do everything; we play a major role in co-laboring with God, working with Him. If you are a person who knows what God has called you to do and you're sitting on it, know that obedience is greater than sacrifice. It's time to make your move, take the step and command the spirit of fear to get under your feet. Don't allow anything to get in your way from bringing God the Glory! So rise up, you are Purpose Unstoppable!

~ Scripture to Memorize ~

Memorize the scripture below; I believe it will help you know that God already had a plan created for you before sending you here on earth and He has some great things in store for you!

"For I know the plans I have for you," says the LORD. "They are plans for good and not for disaster, to give you a future and a hope."

Jeremiah 29:11 (NLT)

~ Chapter Scriptural Reflections ~

God's Plan for Your Life

For I know the plans I have for you," declares the LORD, "plans to prosper you and not to harm you, plans to give you hope and a future.

Jeremiah 29:11 (NIV)

The human body has many parts, but the many parts make up one whole body. So it is with the body of Christ.

1 Corinthians 12:12 (NLT)

Even before he made the world, God loved us and chose us in Christ to be holy and without fault in his eyes

Ephesians 1:4(NLT)

"Before I formed you in the womb I knew you, before you were born I set you apart; I appointed you as a prophet to the nations."

Jeremiah 1:5 (NIV)

Persistency

Keep on asking, and you will receive what you ask for. Keep on seeking, and you will find. Keep on knocking, and the door will be opened to you.

Matthew 7:7(NLT)

Therefore I tell you, whatever you ask for in prayer, believe that you have received it, and it will be yours.

Mark 11:24 (NIV)

It's Time to Make Your Move

You will seek me and find me when you seek me with all your heart.

Jeremiah 29:13 (NLT)

"When everything appears to be going wrong, still trust God, because it is not what it seems."

~Tiffany M. Hill

5

Embracing the Process by Trusting God

~ Proverbs 3:5-6 (NLT) ~

Trust in the LORD with all your heart; do not depend on your own understanding. Seek his will in all you do, and he will show you which path to take.

As we continue to walk with God, I've learned that He will place us in temporary situations to teach us to trust Him and to show Himself strong in our lives. When God is taking us through a process of teaching us how to trust Him in any situation, it can be a painful experience. It can at times appear that everything is going wrong, but in those moments we must know that God is with us through it all and that He's in control. I experienced having to embrace the process that God was taking me through, specifically in the area of my professional career, serving children and families. However, after working for 10 years, I began to experience a backwards momentum regarding my job positions. I went from being in higher performing leadership roles to positions that I progressed far beyond, going backwards to where I initially began in my career. Throughout this journey, I would often ask the Lord, what's going on? Why do I have to go backwards instead of staying in the position where I was? It was humiliating to endure the backwards momentum. I was upset and couldn't understand what was happening during that time. As the decline continued to occur, I was faced with persecution and was terminated from my job. Now, it was nothing I did to cause the unexpected termination to occur. I knew the Lord allowed this to happen, because nothing happens without God's approval. I recall walking in the door to work before being terminated and the Lord led me to read Ephesians 6: 11-17 (NIV) - The Armor of God.

"Put on the full armor of God, so that you can take your stand against the devil's schemes. For our struggle is not against flesh and blood, but against the rulers, against the authorities, against the powers of this dark world and against the spiritual forces of evil in the heavenly realms. Therefore put on the full armor of God, so that when the day of evil comes, you may be able to stand your ground. Stand firm then, with the belt of truth buckled around your waist, with the breastplate of righteousness in place, and with your feet fitted with the readiness that comes from the gospel of peace. In addition to all this, take up the shield of faith, with which you can extinguish all the flaming arrows of the evil one. Take the helmet of salvation and the sword of the Spirit, which is the word of God."

Shortly after reading that scripture, I was called into a room where I was informed of the unexpected termination; in that moment, I began to feel the peace of God cover me. I was in a supernatural peace bubble; nothing that occurred affected me emotionally. I had to embrace the process that He was taking me through even though I had never experienced this level of learning to trust God.

After experiencing job loss, I went to the unemployment office. Being in the unemployment office was a very humbling experience. I began to ask the Lord, how in the world, did I get here? I was immediately at a loss for words. As I stood there, feeling discouraged by the reality that was directly in my face and around me, the Lord showed me in a vision. He and I were walking on water. As I began to follow Him, I looked to my left and right. He said these are called distractions, if you keep your eyes on me, you will not fall. When the vision ended, I remember feeling an overwhelming sense of peace that gave me courage and strength to step over what was going on around me as I continued to move forward through the pain of it all.

In going through this process, I learned that trusting God to this magnitude was not very easy. God allowed me to see Him differently; He showed me how to completely trust Him for everything, as He continued to sustain my family. I did not know what was going to happen next in my situation, but I continued to praise and worship Him through it all. God deserves our praise, not only when life is going well, but during the hard and difficult times that we face in our lives as well. When we trust God our dependency is on Him, not on ourselves. We are confident and certain that He will come through for us. He has brought us out of situations time and time again. That's why we cannot depend on our own understanding; we must allow God to take us on the path that He set before us by trusting Him. Romans 5:3-4 (NLT) says "We can rejoice, too, when we run into problems and trials, for we know that they help us develop endurance. And endurance develops strength of character, and character strengthens our confident hope of salvation." As we grow in God and embrace the process when enduring challenging circumstances in our lives, it allows us to draw closer to Him in our relationship. It also allows us to develop our character, so that we can be fully developed, prepared and ready to receive our next great thing from Him. God wants us to be able to trust Him, not only when things are going well in our lives, but He wants us to trust Him in times when we are unsure of the next step to take.

I encourage you to trust God in whatever you may be facing in your life, no matter what it looks like around you, or how painful it may feel. If you've experienced a backwards momentum, look at it as a sling shot;

in the Kingdom of God we go down before going up. God is pulling you back to propel and push you forward to your next level of greatness. If you're facing a situation that you've never faced before and you're trying to find God in it, "don't focus on the negative by looking down, but rather, search for the light by looking towards Jesus Christ"~Bishop Dale C. Bonner. God knows what He's doing and He loves and cares for us so trust the process that He's taking you through. I'm rooting for you!

Guard Your Heart

~ Proverbs 4:23 (NIV) ~

Above all else, guard your heart,
for everything you do flows from it.

As I continued trusting God, I couldn't allow the backwards momentum; the persecution and job loss limit my continued growth in God. It was important for me to protect and guard my heart as a gatekeeper. This meant I had to be in control of what I allowed to enter in and affect me; such as the feelings of anger and bitterness towards others. As Proverbs 4:23 says, "Above all else, guard your heart, for everything you do flows from it." In my revelation of this scripture, God is referring to our non-tangible heart, which is our mind (thoughts), emotions (feelings) and will (choices). If we can neglect our physical heart by not properly caring for ourselves physically, then for sure we can neglect our non-physical, intangible heart, which is the inner core of who we are. Our feelings can get the best of us as we experience life's circumstances, they can sometimes take us for a ride, causing unforgiving and bitterness to settle within our hearts. Mark 11:25 (NIV) states, "And when you stand praying, if you hold anything against anyone, forgive them, so that your Father in heaven may forgive you your sins." We must let it go, by releasing and giving it to God in prayer; forgive, then move on.

The way we feel can also lead to negative thoughts, but do not focus on negative thoughts. Philippians 4:8 (NIV) says "Finally, brothers and sisters, whatever is true, whatever is noble, whatever is right, whatever is pure, whatever is lovely, whatever is admirable–if anything is excellent or praiseworthy–think about such things."

If you're not thinking on those things mentioned in the scripture, then your thoughts are not aligned with the word of God, and your thoughts do not have the right to run rampant in your mind. When a negative thought arises, immediately take authority and arrest that thought and speak words of encouragement or scripture out loud to make it obedient to Christ. In 2 Corinthians 10:5 (NIV), it states "We demolish arguments and every pretension that sets itself up against the knowledge of God, and we take captive every thought to make it obedient to Christ." For example, your thought may be, 'I'm discouraged and God has nothing good for me.' You then immediately counteract that thought with, 'God you are good, your plans for me are for my good and not to cause me any harm.' Your feelings can lead to a thought, which leads to a decision. The Lord gave us our own will so that we can decide between what's right and wrong. You have the power of choice. If you do not make the right choices, in most cases it can affect the outcome of your situation. You should always consult God to lead you in making the right choices by the Holy Spirits leading.

~ Casting your thoughts challenge ~

No one is perfect, we all have negative thoughts. But the next time you have a negative thought, immediately cast it down with positive words or a scripture (talk back to it). I'm excited for your growth!

Search My Heart

~ Psalm 139:23-24 (NLT) ~

Search me, O God, and know my heart; test me and know my anxious thoughts. Point out anything in me that offends you, and lead me along the path of everlasting life.

When I lost my job, I had to ask God to remove anything that did not represent Him. I did not want any hindrances of negativity to enter into my heart. When dealing with matters of the heart, it is important to ask God, in prayer, to search and purify our hearts of anything that is not of Him. We want to be intentional in representing Jesus Christ. In our actions and attitude towards others, while also being truthful to ourselves with the Lord in prayer. With this, God begins to reveal and remove the things that we have submitted to Him and places us on the right path. When things are going on in your life and you can't figure out how you arrived in this foreign land, just remember God hasn't left you. During this test you have to trust the process of where God is taking you. Stay connected with the Lord in prayer and in worship, as this is where your relationship is birthed. He will give you the strength you need to make it through.

As you ponder on Proverbs 4:23 (NIV), "Above all else, guard your heart, for everything you do flows from it." Know that it is extremely important, to go before the Lord often to ask for Him to search and purify your heart. Our heart is what connects us to God and to people that are very important to us. If our hearts are polluted, then that's what comes up and out. The pollution affects our thoughts, words, actions and direction and can ultimately limit our growth in all areas of our lives

Resting in the Lord

~ *Matthew 11:28 (NIV)* ~

Come to me, all you who are weary and burdened, and I will give you rest.

When we are faced with challenging situations in our lives, our feelings and emotions can be a heavy load to carry. As we trust God, that load becomes extremely light once we hand it over to the Lord. As I mentioned earlier in this chapter, I lost my job, but after that, things began to happen in a domino effect, one thing after the other. I continued to look to God for the peace and rest that I needed, because I couldn't focus in on the things going on around me. The Lord led me to Matthew 11:28 (NIV), which states "Come to me, all you who are weary and burdened, and I will give you rest." The scripture tell us that we were not created to carry a heavy load of worry, anxiety, pain, or discouragement. Our Lord and Savior Jesus Christ paid the price on the cross with the shedding of His blood, to release us from having to carry all of our burdens.

Since the word of God promises rest to us in dealing with circumstances and situations that we face, we must literally, hand over to God all of our cares and burdens. Once we've handed our cares over to the Lord, we do not have the right to pick them back up, because we do not own them anymore. So, here's how I give my cares over to the Lord, when dealing with the situation I was faced with. I would cuff both of my hands up to my mouth and speak my concern into my hands out loud. I then remove my hands from my mouth while my hands remain cuffed and I take my hand to give it over to God. This helped me in giving what I was carrying to God. I encourage you to try it before ending this chapter.

As you give your heavy load over to the Lord, know that it is not easy to do. I believe it takes continuous practice, intentionality, faith, and being truthful with yourself and God in order for you to have, in return, Gods promise of rest. I remember having to sit down to be very honest with myself as to the real reasons why I wasn't handing my burdens and cares over to the Lord. I had to truthfully answer some questions. Do I trust God? Do I believe God to be faithful to His word by fulfilling His promise? My response to those questions was "YES!" I made the decision to trust God by fully handing my burdens and cares over to the Lord. I recommend you sit down, by yourself, and make a list of reasons why you're not handing your cares and burdens over to the Lord. This will help you identify the possible limitations of the promise of rest, and set you free.

When God promises rest, we no longer have sleepless nights. We have a peace of mind, even though all craziness may be happening around us. Even if that is the case, know that God is working it all out in your favor. Here's my testimony of how God showed up in my life after handing my burdens and cares over to Him. I was in His resting bubble during the challenging time I was faced with when I lost my job. There was a leak in my home and this leak wasn't a small leak, it was a leak to be really concerned about. My Husband called the plumber out to fix the leak. After evaluating the problem, it was determined that they had to dig holes in the ground to fix it, but there was one dilemma. The leak could not be fixed that day due to the rain; they would have to return the following week to make the repair. Upon reassessing the leak, it was determined that the repair could be made from the inside, without having to do any costly digging. As a result, they left us with a fixed pipe and a $0 balance. Praise God! The Lord delivered on His promise to me during this entire situation. I was not agitated or concerned, I found rest instead. If God delivered on His promises to me, He will certainly give you the rest He promises for you. God loves you and He will never ever leave you.

~ Try these helpful habits while waiting on your Promise of Rest ~

I've provided a few helpful habits that helped me in handing my cares and burdens over to the Lord to receive the promise of rest in the Lord. I am confident it will help you as well. I encourage you to write them down as a reference when you're facing challenging situations.

1. Pray, Praise & Worship God while in and out of your situation
2. Try not to think about your situation
3. Stay motivated by listening to uplifting music
4. Keep people out of your ear, who oppose your belief
5. Declare the word of the Lord often over your situation
6. Remind yourself of who God is and what God has already done
7. Keep a positive attitude
8. Don't be moved or shaken, stay and remain focused
9. Don't talk about it and do not apologize or feel guilty for not discussing your situation with others
10. Take authority and arrest any negative thoughts with scripture or positive words

Allow God to be God

~ Deuteronomy 32:4 (NLT) ~

He is the Rock; his deeds are perfect. Everything he does is just and fair. He is a faithful God who does no wrong; how just and upright he is!

Learning to allow God to be God in our lives is certainly easier said than done. We tend to think we can step right in and handle things the way we see fit. We sometimes take matters into our own hands, by allowing our emotions to get the best of us or we listen to what others are saying around us and that makes us move without God. But as we are maturing and growing in God we must believe and stand on His word knowing Him to be faithful in our lives. This means that we give up total control and allow Him to take over in our situations; even if it takes months or maybe even years to receive what we are trusting and believing God for in our lives. Deuteronomy 32:4 (NLT), states, in part, "He is the Rock; his deeds are perfect. Everything he does is just and fair. He is a faithful God who does no wrong." We serve a faithful God and He was faithful in delivering on His promise to me. I was vindicated after being terminated from my job; I trusted and believed God for His promise that He is my defender. He did just that, without me having to defend myself. Praise God, right here!

Waiting on the promises of God is a faith move. If God has given us instructions, to wait on our promise by not taking matters into our own hands, then we are moving by faith in responding to what God is requiring of us. In your waiting, you may be waiting on vindication, as I was, or for God to bring restoration to your life or family. In whatever we may be waiting on, as we are waiting, we experience those thoughts or questions that play randomly in our minds about why is it taking so long to happen? We may deal with different emotions of feeling excited because we're really looking forward to receiving our promise from God, or feel as though nothing is happening. It may be painful, tough or discouraging sometimes or feel as though you want to quit and throw in the towel. But, can I tell you not to give up and quit? These feelings are normal when in a position of waiting. I had to face some of these same emotions, but God brought me closer to Him in those moments and I rested in Him, knowing that everything was going to work out the way He wanted it too. Galatians 6:9 (NIV) says "Let us not become weary in doing good, for at the proper time we will reap a harvest if we do not give up." Your harvest will be on time. When I received my promise of vindication, it was on time and well needed. I didn't think about the pain of what I faced in my waiting, it was all a distant memory. I received the news and praised God for being faithful.

While waiting, we cannot focus on those thoughts and feelings because they keep us all over the place and they keep us off focus; not realizing what God is teaching us in the process of waiting. Romans 5:3-4(NLT), states "We can rejoice, too, when we run into problems and trials, for we know that they help us develop endurance. And endurance develops strength of character, and character strengthens our confident hope of salvation." The dictionary definition of the word endurance is to have the power to withstand something challenging; another word for endurance is patience. We cannot skip over the process of endurance and enter into the promises of God; it is not complete without endurance. For instance, a professional athlete cannot skip over the training process to win the game. When we try to skip over the process of endurance in our waiting, then we become impatient and make what we want to happen without God's endorsement. Abraham and Sarah, in the book of Genesis, waited on the promise of a baby from God for 25 years. Sarah took matters into her own hands and had her maid Hagar conceive a child with her Husband. If Sarah would've waited on God to deliver on His promise, as He did, she would not have experienced unnecessary drama between her and Hagar. We serve a faithful God and if we wait and endure to the end, trusting in Him by giving Him total control of our lives, we will not end up in messy situations. I encourage you to wait on God, because the waiting is worth it on the other side of receiving the promise.

~ Serenity Prayer ~

Father God,
God grant me the serenity to accept the things I cannot change; courage to change the things I can; and wisdom to know the difference. Living one day at a time; Enjoying one moment at a time; Accepting hardships as the pathway to peace; Taking, as He did, this sinful world as it is, not as I would have it; Trusting that He will make all things right if I surrender to His Will; That I may be reasonably happy in this life and supremely happy with Him. In Jesus' name Amen.

Retrieved from allaboutprayer.org

~ Chapter Scriptural Reflections ~

Embrace the Process by Trusting God

Trust in the LORD with all your heart; do not depend on your own understanding. Seek his will in all you do, and he will show you which path to take.

Proverbs 3:5-6 (NLT)

"We can rejoice too, when we run into problems and trials, for we know that they help us develop endurance. And endurance develops strength of character, and character strengthens our confident hope of salvation.

Romans 5:3-4 (NLT)

Guard Your Heart

Above all else, guard your heart, for everything you do flows from it.

Proverbs 4:23 (NIV)

"And when you stand praying, if you hold anything against anyone, forgive them, so that your Father in heaven may forgive you your sins."

Mark 11:25 (NIV)

Finally, brothers and sisters, whatever is true, whatever is noble, whatever is right, whatever is pure, whatever is lovely, whatever is admirable–if anything is excellent or praiseworthy–think about such things.

Philippians 4:8 (NIV)

We demolish arguments and every pretension that sets itself up against the knowledge of God, and we take captive every thought to make it obedient to Christ.

2 Corinthians 10:5 (NIV)

Search My Heart

Search me, O God, and know my heart; test me and know my anxious thoughts. Point out anything in me that offends you, and lead me along the path of everlasting life.

Psalm 139:23-24 (NLT)

Resting in the Lord

Come to me, all you who are weary and burdened, and I will give you rest.

Matthew 11:28 (NIV)

Allow God to be God

He is the Rock; his deeds are perfect. Everything he does is just and fair. He is a faithful God who does no wrong; how just and upright he is!

Deuteronomy 32:4 (NLT)

Let us not become weary in doing good, for at the proper time we will reap a harvest if we do not give up.

Galatians 6:9 (NIV)

We can rejoice, too, when we run into problems and trials, for we know that they help us develop endurance. And endurance develops strength of character, and character strengthens our confident hope of salvation.

Romans 5:3-4 (NLT)

"Make a commitment to follow Jesus Christ by surrendering your life, it isn't easy but it's worth it"

~Tiffany M. Hill

6

Making Your Commitment

~ Matthew 16:24-25 (KJV) ~

Then said Jesus unto his disciples, If any man will come after me, let him deny himself, and take up his cross, and follow me. For whosoever will save his life shall lose it: and whosoever will lose his life for my sake shall find it.

After my awakening, people around me couldn't understand, how, by this one experience with God, my whole life was turned around so quickly. But for me, I wasn't focused on the time frame. I knew that by this experience, I wanted God more and more and my mind was made up that I was following Jesus Christ, no matter the cost or what anyone said. I had to deny myself, my life was no longer my life, and it was now His life. When we are not committed and surrendered to God, it is as if we're saying to God I don't want you and what you have for me, but I want me and what I want for me. When we commit and surrender our lives to Jesus Christ we have to give to Him all that we are, have and wanted to become. In return, we get all that He is, to do His will for the advancement of His Kingdom. This is what I signed up for and I am committed and have surrendered my life to follow Jesus Christ.

In being committed to following Jesus Christ, I stepped out on faith, responding to what God required of me as to the calling on my life. I made the decision not to return to work after the position was re-offered to me. I decided to follow Jesus Christ and not look back in obtaining employment. In making that decision, my faith and trust in God grew to another level. I had to believe and trust God for provision much differently than when I depended on a consistent, bi-weekly pay check. As I faced having difficult conversations with the people I loved, they didn't quite understand my decision. A job was customary where I come from, other than having a secular business for financial resources. I trusted God and believed the promises that He made to me and I made a decision to step out on faith and not look back, I was all in.

In being totally committed to God, as Christians, we must be willing to step out on faith completely and entirely trusting God, even when it surpasses our understanding with whatever He's instructing us to do. It may be from a promise revealed to us in God's word, which is loaded with His promises, or a personal promise we heard from the Lord. Either way, we must step out on faith to believe God when it appears to be risky, and even when God hasn't given us all the information, because, to be honest, if we knew everything we wouldn't need trust.

In Hebrews 11:1(KJV) the scripture talks about having "Now" faith, and now faith is the substance of things hoped for; it is the evidence of things not seen. The word substance is something tangible and solid that we're looking for and hoping for God to manifest in our life. We cannot see it or feel it with our five senses; we have it, it's ours, because it's a promise, but we do not posses it in the natural. Therefore, it is important to believe before receiving a promise from God. The bible says, without faith it is impossible to please God. As Christians, we want to always be pleasing to the Lord by having faith. When we do not believe, it is as if we are saying that God is not real and His promise is not true. Which we know is far from the truth. He is not a man that would lie and He is absolutely the true and living God. The one thing about faith that one must know, is that faith is movement and action towards the promise of God. Therefore, I had to act on my faith by making an actual move, I went after the promise that God had given me in order for my promise to be made manifest. But here's the thing, faith is firm and unmovable, I had to stand on that particular promise by having now faith. This is not based upon our emotions, conversation or a thought in our mind that stays there. It is making a move to be all in by responding to God with faith.

I encourage you to commit to God and go after the promises of God. If you're not sure that you have heard from the Lord, continue pressing in to God through prayer and with fasting. Also know that there's safety in a multitude of counselors, Proverbs 11:14 (KJV), so seek wise counsel and pray with someone. When going after your promises, know that others may or may not agree, don't give up, you have to be strong in the Lord and be okay with those who do not agree with your moving by faith. Faith is trusting in something that you can't even prove; no one can see it, because it hasn't even manifested itself yet. It is always in response to what God requires. It may seem strange to others around you, but that may be because their level of faith isn't the same as your level of faith. If this is the case, God can use you in that area to encourage or provoke them to believe in Him just as you do, all for His glory.

Walking in Boldness

~ 2 Timothy 1:7 (KJV) ~

For God hath not given us the spirit of fear; but of power, and of love, and of a sound mind

Being all in and committed to God, requires us to walk in boldness, by stepping over fear. When making the decision to step out on faith to follow Jesus Christ, the enemy told me all kinds of lies. He said that I was going to lose everything that I had ever owned. But after sitting and pondering on what the devil said, I broke out of the fear and I started to talk back to the devil. I commanded him to get under my feet by the power and the authority of the Holy Spirit. After breaking out of the fear,

I recall experiencing this feeling of freedom, as if I had broken out of the jail of my thoughts and looked and believed God for the impossible in my life. Fear is doubt, terror, panic, worry, and concern (this list goes on and on). 2 Timothy 1:7 (KJV) states "For God hath not given us the spirit of fear; but of power, and of love and of sound mind." Fear is not of God, it is a spirit and it attacks us through people and the circumstances that we my face. When it attaches itself to us, it can paralyze us in our moving in faith towards the promises of God.

When Peter was on the boat with the disciples, he saw Jesus walking on water. He asked Jesus Christ if he could come out to Him and walk on water. As he began walking, fear began to come up against him from the waves and the winds and Peter got back inside of the boat. Now, when Peter got back on the boat, this said to me that he focused on the lies from the enemy or what was happening around him from the waves and the winds instead of keeping his eyes focused on Jesus. Faith was telling Peter, as he got out of the boat, to come to Jesus. He can trust God to be faithful to His promises no matter what it may look like or what the enemy is saying to him. However fear was telling Peter, to get back on the boat because the situation looked too hard to conquer. Fear becomes an issue in our lives, if we allow it to keep us from moving. Fear can keep us from ever reaching our fullest potential. That means we can never discover what God has placed on the inside of us, to inspire the world around us. God has great things for us to do and we cannot allow the spirit of fear to intimidate us in fulfilling our assignment on earth.

God did not give us fear; He gave us boldness through His Spirit that indwells in us, which is power, love and a sound mind. He gave us power which means authority, force and strength to command fear to leave and get under our feet. He gave us love; 1 John 4:18 (NIV) says "There is no fear in love. But perfect love drives out fear, because fear has to do with punishment. The one who fears is not made perfect in love." God is love; He wouldn't place us in circumstances to harm us. If you're experiencing fear in any situation or relationship, know that this is not of God.

We have a sound mind, meaning we have an understanding of who God is, and if He's given us a promise we can expect that He is faithful to deliver on it to us. There is a reason why the enemy fights us with fear because he doesn't want us to win. If you're experiencing fear in any area in your life, submit it to God and move in faith over fear. Don't allow fear to stop your movement by faith in getting what God has promised to you.

Self-Discipline

~ 1 Corinthians 9:24-27 (NIV) ~

Do you not know that in a race all the runners run, but only one gets the prize? Run in such a way as to get the prize. Everyone who competes in the games goes into strict training. They do it to get a crown that will not last, but we do it to get a crown that will last forever. Therefore I do not run like someone running aimlessly; I do not fight like a boxer beating the air. No, I strike a blow to my body and make it my slave so that after I have preached to others, I myself will not be disqualified for the prize.

The Dictionary of Bible Themes defines discipline as *"Loving and corrective training that leads to maturity and responsibility on the part of those who experience it."* Self-discipline plays a huge role in growing with God. It is a process for ensuring we experience the next level in our lives that God wants for us, in all areas of our life. After stepping out on faith to follow Jesus Christ, I had to become more disciplined to be faithful and responsible towards the things of God. Therefore, I had to incorporate a regimen while at home, to remain accountable while also eliminating outside distractions. I was willing to endure self-denial to, in turn, receive more of God.

If we are not disciplining ourselves it affects every area of our life; such as our money, thoughts, relationships, personal care etc. When we wake up each day with a lack of order in our lives, we cannot be successful. Think about an athlete's self disciplined lifestyle. They pay tons of money to train in order to keep their bodies healthy, to be successful, in order for them to receive a prize of victory in return by receiving a trophy, which is temporary. As Christians, how much more should we become disciplined spiritually to receive, in return, a crown of eternal blessings?

As I have continued to grow in God, I realized that it becomes easier to self- discipline ourselves when we have clear vision of our purpose. Having purpose keeps us focused and directed towards the one thing that God has called us to do. When we have no clear direction from God about His will for our lives, it keeps us unnecessarily busy and confused with broad options, making it more difficult to refuse distractions. Distractions can come to us in the form of people and also from our environment. If we're not determined in being self-disciplined, those distractions can lead us where it wants to take us and, before we know it, we are unable to reach our goal in growing with God. I encourage you to become self-disciplined, be determined and persistent, despite any opposition you may face, while doing the things of God. We always want to give God our best, all for His glory.

~ Make a digital schedule and stick to it ~

In order for me to stay on task and remain self-disciplined, I use my phone's calendar or alarm clock. I then label the notification to inform me as to what's next. This helps me stay on task and focused. As you continue with this strategy, eventually you won't need it as your body and mind becomes trained due to repetition. I pray that this helps you in becoming self-disciplined for God.

~ Chapter Scriptural Reflections~

Making Your Commitment

Then said Jesus unto his disciples, If any man will come after me, let him deny himself, and take up his cross, and follow me. For whosoever will save his life shall lose it: and whosoever will lose his life for my sake shall find it.

Matthew 16:24-25 (KJV)

*Now faith is the substance of things hoped for;
the evidence of things not seen.*

Hebrews 11:1(KJV)

Where no counsel is, the people fall: but in the multitude of counselors there is safety.

Proverbs 11:14 (KJV)

Walking in Boldness

For God hath not given us the spirit of fear; but of power and of love and a sound mind

2 Timothy 1:7 (KJV)

There is no fear in love. But perfect love drives out fear, because fear has to do with punishment. The one who fears is not made perfect in love.

1 John 4:18 (NIV)

Self-Discipline

Do you not know that in a race all the runners run, but only one gets the prize? Run in such a way as to get the prize. Everyone who competes in the games goes into strict training. They do it to get a crown that will not last, but we do it to get a crown that will last forever. Therefore I do not run like someone running aimlessly; I do not fight like a boxer beating the air. No, I strike a blow to my body and make it my slave so that after I have preached to others, I myself will not be disqualified for the prize.

1 Corinthians 9:24-27 (NIV)

"We will never know what God placed on the inside of us to share with the world if we don't start by taking action to stir up our gifts."

~Tiffany M. Hill

7

Taking Action

~ *1 Peter 4:10 (NIV)* ~

Each of you should use whatever gift you have received to serve others, as faithful stewards of God's grace in its various forms.

When God changed and transformed my life, I knew within my spirit that I had to take action to serve God by serving others. I started serving in my local community and also in several ministries at my church. Serving others was nothing new for me prior to my experience. However, this particular time after my awakening, I served having had an experience with God and also with knowledge and wisdom from Gods word when serving others. I would serve others on my job starting with the people around me. As I continued serving, I started my first ministry in my home, praying and teaching the word of God to my family through weekly Bible studies. I would also minister and pray for people around me on my job. I wanted to share Jesus with everyone, but it started right where I was.

As believers, we are the hands and feet of Jesus. We serve others just as Jesus did, with love and joy in our hearts, never placing ourselves in a position higher than others. In John 13:15 (NIV) Jesus said, "I have set you an example that you should do as I have done for you." Jesus is our example; He served and taught the disciple's through His actions and the word of God. Serving is not to be kept just within our church doors, but we must serve everywhere we are.

There are many ways in which we can serve Jesus by serving others. I've listed a few suggestions to serve, encouraging you to take action, if not already. But first, we will review the motivational gifts which are our serving gifts.

Referenced from The Institute in Basic Life Principles:

Motivational Gifts - (Romans 12:6-8), there are seven motivational gifts that God placed into us and are to be used to serve one another for the glory of God. Everyone has a motivational gift. A motivational gift can be compared to a set of eyeglasses from God, given so that the believer can see people and circumstances through that particular set of "lenses." I've listed descriptions of the seven motivational gifts, explaining how a person with each gift would "see" his or her role in the Body of Christ.

Speaking Gifts

- *Prophecy:* also can be referred to as simple prophecy. In Greek prophecy means a speaking forth. This gift does not foretell the future. But, it strengthens comforts and encourages others. Note: There are many layers to prophecy.
- *Teacher: r*esearch and communicate complicated truths, they keep the body of Christ studying and learning the word of God.
- *Exhorter*: enjoys encouraging others, they are very positive; they counsel others and help the body of Christ to apply spiritual truths.

Serving Gifts

- *Serving:* gift of servitude, loves to serve others they keep the body of Christ moving.
- *Giver:* love to give money, time, talent and energy in order to meet needs, give without regrets.

- *Administrator:* organize, lead, direct, and facilitate, to show the body of Christ how to increase in our vision.
- Mercy: shows compassion and provides personal and emotional support love and care to those in need. Immune to error.

Suggestions for serving God by serving others;

Serve God by serving children-Luke 18:16 (NIV) But Jesus called the children to him and said, "Let the little children come to me, and do not hinder them, for the kingdom of God belongs to such as these.

- Volunteer by reading books to children in local schools
- Volunteer in your church to care for the children during service or other activities.

Serve God by giving and visiting those in need -Matthew 25:34-36 (NIV) "Then the King will say to those on his right, 'Come, you who are blessed by my Father; take your inheritance, the kingdom prepared for you since the creation of the world. For I was hungry and you gave me something to eat, I was thirsty and you gave me something to drink, I was a stranger and you invited me in, I needed clothes and you clothed me, I was sick and you looked after me, I was in prison and you came to visit me.'

- Giving the tithe and offering.
- Volunteer at local shelters in your area to serve food, clean etc.
- Donate clothing, toiletries etc. items to local shelters
- Create an organization for giving opportunities (Holiday meals etc.)
- Participate in random acts of kindness (open the door for others, randomly purchase food for the next person in line at

a fast food restaurant, purchase a meal for a person in need etc.)

- Join a prison ministry to minister in the prisons.
- Visit and pray for the sick, request the sick and shut in list from church to pray or visit your local Hospital or Nursing Home.

Serve God by caring and supporting others - James 1:27 (NIV) "Religion that God our Father accepts as pure and faultless is this: to look after orphans and widows in their distress and to keep oneself from being polluted by the world."

- Offer to purchase breakfast, lunch or dinner.
- Offer to complete chores (washing clothes, washing dishes etc.)
- Consider adopting a child in need of a family.

Serve God by using your gifts - 1 Peter 4:10-11(NIV) "Each of you should use whatever gift you have received to serve others, as faithful stewards of God's grace in its various forms. If anyone speaks, they should do so as one who speaks the very words of God. If anyone serves, they should do so with the strength God provides, so that in all things God may be praised through Jesus Christ. To him be the glory and the power for ever and ever. Amen."

- Motivational Gifts
- Ministry Gifts
- Manifestation Gifts

I encourage you to take action to Serve God by serving others with love and joy in your heart. Start with people in your midst, God created us to not only live for ourselves, but to share with the world around us our gifts and talents.

Stir Up the Gift

~ 2 Timothy 1:6 (NIV) ~

For this reason I remind you to fan into flame the gift of God, which is in you through the laying on of my hands

God led me to stir up my gifts by starting with my Purpose Unstoppable podcast in September 2018, located on Podbean.com and Apple iTunes. I did not know all that I had in me until I began speaking, as He would give me what to say. I also taught a small Bible study group class and I would practice speaking alone and with my Husband and children. Now my gift has begun making room for me as I am speaking and ministering the gospel to God's people as He opens the doors.

God placed a gift on the inside of you to share with the world and not keep it to yourself. If you're still living and breathing on earth, then there's still something more for you to do. No matter your age, it is never too late to stir up the gift that God has given you. Paul was telling Timothy (2 Timothy 1:6) to stir up the gift that God had placed inside of him to share with the world. There are people waiting to hear from you, but it takes the power of your choice (will), with the help of the Holy Spirit, for you to step out of fear and comfort to do what you're called to do. You will never know the gift that you have until you start moving into the direction of the Holy Spirits leading. If you allow fear and comfort to paralyze you from moving into the direction that God is calling you, then your gift will lie dormant. This means that no one will ever experience your gift and you would never know how your gift was to be used while on earth.

You are not here by accident and you are not a mistake, everything that you've been through, God can use it for His glory, nothing is ever wasted with God. He chose you for a special assignment for good works to serve and worship Him. No longer are you to be like the world and do as the world does, because God has separated you. You're supposed to be different! Doing something different is accepting the calling on your life and stirring up your gift; deciding, moving and doing, equals taking action. No longer are you to wait on others to tell you who God is to you, or even sit on the side lines watching for what's to come next, allowing your purpose to pass you by. It's time, to know Him for yourself and walk into what He has for you.

Some of you may know what God has called you to do and you're afraid and ashamed, you're scared of what others may think about you. But God is not ashamed of you and He hasn't given you the spirit of fear. He's given you power and authority over fear and he approved and confirmed you. If God is for you, who can be against you, says Romans 8:31, so Trust Him! Step out of your fear and shame to do what God has called you to do for the building of his kingdom. Time is not on your side; God's plan for you starts now. Chase after God like never before and seek him with all of your heart. God wants an intimate relationship with you and He has great things in store for you. Began stirring up your gifts by putting them to use starting where you are, bringing Glory to God! Be Purpose Unstoppable.

~Your Dear God Letter~

Take out a piece of paper and pen.

I would like to encourage you to write a rededication letter to God from the depths of your heart. It is a letter of refocusing your relationship with Jesus Christ. Pour out everything to Him and do not stop writing until you feel you have nothing else to say. I believe He wants to hear from you.

~ Chapter Scriptural Reflections~

Taking Action

Each of you should use whatever gift you have received to serve others, as faithful stewards of God's grace in its various forms.

~1 Peter 4:10 (NIV) ~

I have set you an example that you should do as I have done for you.

John 13:15 (NIV)

But Jesus called the children to him and said, "Let the little children come to me, and do not hinder them, for the kingdom of God belongs to such as these.

Luke 18:16 (NIV)

"Then the King will say to those on his right, 'Come, you who are blessed by my Father; take your inheritance, the kingdom prepared for you since the creation of the world. For I was hungry and you gave me something to eat, I was thirsty and you gave me something to drink, I was a stranger and you invited me in, I needed clothes and you clothed me, I was sick and you looked after me, I was in prison and you came to visit me.'

Matthew 25:34-36 (NIV)

Religion that God our Father accepts as pure and faultless is this: to look after orphans and widows in their distress and to keep oneself from being polluted by the world.

James 1:27 (NIV)

Each of you should use whatever gift you have received to serve others, as faithful stewards of God's grace in its various forms. If anyone speaks, they should do so as one who speaks the very words of God. If anyone serves, they should do so with the strength God provides, so that in all things God may be praised through Jesus Christ. To him be the glory and the power for ever and ever. Amen.

1 Peter 4:10-11(NIV)

Stir Up the Gift

For this reason I remind you to fan into flame the gift of God, which is in you through the laying on of my hands

2 Timothy 1:6 (NIV)

What, then, shall we say in response to these things? If God is for us, who can be against us?

Romans 8:31 (NIV)

Made in the USA
Columbia, SC
27 October 2020

23492282R00063